SELF-ENQUIRY

'VICHARA SANGRAHAM' OF
BHAGAVAN SRI RAMANA MAHARSHI

TRANSLATED FROM THE ORIGINAL TAMIL
by DR T·M·P· MAHADEVAN, M.A., Ph.D.

Sri Ramanasramam
Tiruvannamalai
INDIA

SELF-ENQUIRY (English).
Original work in Tamil: *Vicāra Saṅgraham* by Bhagavan Sri Ramana Maharshi
Translated by Dr. T.M.P. Mahadevan
© Sri Ramanasramam, Tiruvannamalai

Twelfth Edition	:	*1999*	*— 2000 copies*
Thirteenth Edition	:	*2003*	*— 2000 copies*
Fourteenth Edition	:	*2005*	*— 2000 copies*
Fifteenth Edition	:	*2008*	*— 2000 copies*
Sixteenth Edition	:	*2010*	*— 2000 copies*
Seventeenth Edition	:	*2013*	*— 2000 copies*
Eighteenth Edition	:	*2015*	*— 2000 copies*
Nineteenth Edition	:	*2018*	*— 2000 copies*
Twentieth Edition	:	2021	

2000 copies

CC No. 1043

ISBN: 978-81-88018-55-0

Price: ₹25

Published by
Venkat S. Ramanan
President
Sri Ramanasramam
Tiruvannamalai 606 603
Tamil Nadu, INDIA

Website : www.sriramanamaharshi.org

Typeset at
Sri Ramanasramam

Printed by
Prism Art Press
Chennai 600 028
Tamil Nadu, INDIA

INTRODUCTION

The present work in prose consists of forty questions with answers covering the entire range of spiritual disciplines required for the gaining of release (*moksha*). The questioner was Gambhiram Seshayya, one of the early devotees of Bhagavan Sri Ramana Maharshi. He was a Municipal Overseer at Tiruvannamalai about 1900. Besides being an ardent Ramabhakta (worshipper of Rama) he was interested in the study and practice of *yoga*. He used to read Swami Vivekananda's lectures on the different *yogas* as also an English translation of the *Rama Gita*. For resolving the difficulties which he came across while studying these books and in his spiritual practices, he approached Bhagavan Sri Ramana from time to time. Bhagavan, who was only twenty-one years old, was then living in Virupaksha cave on Arunachala Hill. As he was keeping silent at the time – not because of any vow taken, but because he was not inclined to talk – he wrote out his answers to Seshayya's questions on bits of paper. These writings over the period 1900-1902 were later copied in a notebook by Seshayya. The material thus gathered was published by Sri Ramanasramam under the title *Vichara Sangraham* which literally means 'A Compendium of Self-Enquiry'. A digest of the teaching contained in this work was later printed in English bearing the title 'Self-Enquiry'. In that English version, the questions were omitted and the substance of Bhagavan's teaching was given, classifying it in twelve short chapters with appropriate headings. The present English translation is of the entire original text *Vichara Sangraham* as it is in Tamil. The *Vichara Sangraham* has a unique value in the sense that it constitutes the first set of instructions given by Bhagavan in his own handwriting.

A careful study of the instructions given by Bhagavan here will reveal that they are based on his own plenary experience as confirmed by the sacred texts which were brought to his notice by the early devotees and which he perused for the purpose of clearing the doubts that arose in the minds of the devotees. In the course of his instructions, Bhagavan makes use of such expressions as, 'the scriptures declare', 'thus say the sages', etc. He also cites passages from texts like the *Bhagavad Gita* and the *Viveka Chudamani* and once he mentions by name the *Ribhu Gita*. But it is quite clear that these citations are offered only as confirmations of the truth discovered by Bhagavan himself in his own experience.

The basic teaching is that of *Advaita Vedanta*. The plenary experience of the non-dual Self is the goal; enquiry into the nature of the Self is the means. When the mind identifies the Self with the not-self (the body, etc.), there is bondage; when this wrong identification is removed through the enquiry 'Who am I?' there is release. Thus, Self-enquiry is the direct path taught by Bhagavan Ramana. The 'I'-experience is common to all. Of all thoughts, the 'I'-thought is the first to arise. What one has to do is to enquire into the source of the 'I'-thought. This is the reverse process of what ordinarily happens in the life of the mind. The mind enquires into the constitution and source of everything else which, on examination, will be found to be its own projection; it does not reflect on itself and trace itself to its source. Self-discovery can be achieved by giving the mind an inward turn. This is not to be confused with the introspection of which the psychologists speak. Self-enquiry is not the mind's inspection of its own contents; it is tracing the mind's first mode, the 'I'-thought to its source which is the Self. When there is proper and persistent enquiry, the

'I'-thought also ceases and there is the wordless illumination of the form 'I-I' which is the Pure Consciousness. This is release, freedom from bondage. The method by which this is accomplished, as has been shown, is enquiry which, in *Vedanta*, is termed *jnana* – knowledge. True devotion (*bhakti*), meditation (*dhyana*), and concentration (*yoga*) are identical therewith. As Bhagavan makes it perfectly clear, not to forget the plenary Self-experience is real devotion, mind-control, knowledge, and all other austerities. In the language of devotion, the final goal may be described as the resolution of the mind in its source which is God, the Self, in that of technical *yoga*, it may be described as the dissolution of the mind in the Heart-lotus. These are only different ways of expressing the same truth.

The path of Self-enquiry is found difficult by those who have not acquired the necessary competence for it. The mind should first be rendered pure and one-pointed. This is done through meditation, etc. So, the various paths, in their secondary sense, are auxiliaries to the direct path which is Self-enquiry. In this context, Bhagavan refers to three grades of aspirants: the highest, the medium, and the lowest. For the highest type of aspirants, the path prescribed is *Vedanta* enquiry; through this path, the mind becomes quiescent in the Self and finally ceases to be, leaving the pure Self-experience untarnished and resplendent. The path for the medium is meditation on the Self. Meditation consists in directing a continuous flow of the mind towards the same object. There are several modes of meditation. The best mode is that which is of the form 'I am the Self'. This mode eventually culminates in Self-realisation. For the lowest grade of aspirants, the discipline that is useful is breath-control which in turn results in mind control.

Bhagavan explains the difference between *jnana yoga* (path of knowledge) and *dhyana yoga* (path of meditation) thus: *jnana* is like subduing a self-willed bull by coaxing it with the help of a sheaf of green grass, while *dhyana* is like controlling it by using force. Just as there are eight limbs for *dhyana yoga*, there are eight for *jnana yoga*. The limbs of the latter are more proximate to the final stage than those of the former. For instance, while the *pranayama* of technical *yoga* consists in regulating and restraining breath, the *pranayama* that is a limb of *jnana* relates to rejecting the name-and-form world which is non-real and realising the Real which is Existence-Consciousness-Bliss. *Sat chit annuda*

Realisation of the Self can be gained in this very life. In fact, Self-realisation is not something which is to be gained afresh. We are already the Self; the Self alone is. It is ignorance that makes us imagine that we have not realised the Self. When this ignorance is removed through Self-knowledge, we realise our eternal Self-nature. One who has gained this realisation is called a *jivanmukta* (liberated while living). To others, he may appear to continue to tenant a body. For the benefit of those others it is stated that the body will continue so long as the residue of the *prarabdha karma* (that *karma* of the past which has begun to fructify in the shape of the present body) lasts, and that when the momentum is spent the body will fall and the *jivanmukta* will become a *videhamukta*. But from the standpoint of the Absolute Truth, there is no difference in *mukti*. What needs to be understood is that *mukti* or release is the inalienable nature of the Self.

This, in substance, is Bhagavan Sri Ramana's teaching in the *Vichara Sangraham*.

University of Madras
November 15, 1965.   T.M.P. MAHADEVAN

NOTE TO THE EIGHTH EDITION

The earliest edition of this work in Question-Answer form, I have come across, is dated 1930, published by A. Shivalinga Mudaliyar and V. Subrahmanya Achari and printed at Saravana Bava Press, Madras. This bears a foreword by Muruganar which is dated June 16th, 1930. It is mentioned in the foreword that it was Natanananda that edited the work in Question-Answer form. In his preface, Natanananda observes that the work contains the teachings given in writing by Bhagavan Ramana to Gambhiram Seshayya in the years 1901-1902. It is in the Question-Answer form that this work is included in the *Collected Works* in Tamil, in its early editions, published by the Asramam. In the third edition published in 1940, as well as in subsequent editions, the *Self-Enquiry* appears in the form of a digest. In the footnote that occurs at the end of the Publisher's Note, it is stated that the manuscript copy given by Gambhiram Seshayya's brother was edited by Shivaprakasam Pillai, and was put into Question-Answer form by Natanananda.

Madras
January 18, 1971.   T.M.P. MAHADEVAN

SELF-ENQUIRY
VICHARA SANGRAHAM
of
BHAGAVAN SRI RAMANA MAHARSHI

INVOCATION

Is there any way of adoring the Supreme which is all, except by abiding firmly as that!

1

Disciple: Master! What is the means to gain the state of eternal bliss, ever devoid of misery?

Master: Apart from the statement in the Vedas that wherever there is body there is misery, this is also the direct experience of all people; therefore, one should enquire into one's true nature which is ever bodiless, and one should remain as such. This is the means to gaining that state.

2

D: What is meant by saying that one should enquire into one's true nature and understand it?

M: Experiences such as, 'I went; I came; I was; I did' come naturally to everyone. From these experiences, does it not appear that the consciousness 'I' is the subject of those various acts? Enquiry into the true nature of that consciousness, and remaining as oneself is the way to understand, through enquiry, one's true nature.

3

D: How is one to enquire: 'Who am I?'

M: Actions such as 'going' and 'coming' belong only to the body. And so, when one says, 'I went, I came', it amounts to saying that the body is 'I'. But, can the body be said to be the consciousness 'I', since the body was not before it was born, is made up of the five elements, is non-existent in the state of deep sleep, and becomes a corpse when dead? Can this body which is inert like a log of wood be said to shine as 'I-I'? Therefore, the 'I' consciousness which at first arises in respect of the body is referred to variously as self-conceit (*tarbodham*), egoity (*ahankara*), nescience (*avidya*), *maya*, impurity (*mala*), and individual soul (*jiva*). Can we remain without enquiring into this? Is it not for our redemption through enquiry that all the scriptures declare that the destruction of 'self-conceit' is release (*mukti*)? Therefore, making the corpse-body remain as a corpse, and not even uttering the word 'I', one should enquire keenly thus: "Now, what is it that rises as 'I'?" Then, there would shine in the Heart a kind of wordless illumination of the form 'I-I'. That is, there would shine of its own accord the pure consciousness which is unlimited and one, the limited and the many thoughts having disappeared. If one remains quiescent without abandoning that (experience), the egoity, the individual sense, of the form 'I am the body' will be totally destroyed, and at the end the final thought, viz. the 'I'-form also will be quenched like the fire that burns camphor.* The great sages and scriptures declare that this alone is release.

---

* That is, without leaving any sediment.

4

D: When one enquires into the root of 'self-conceit' which is of the form 'I', all sorts of different thoughts without number seem to rise and not any separate 'I' thought.

M: Whether the nominative case, which is the first case, appears or not, the sentences in which the other cases appear have as their basis the first case; similarly, all the thoughts that appear in the heart have as their basis the egoity which is the first mental mode 'I', the cognition of the form 'I am the body'; thus, it is the rise of egoity that is the cause and source of the rise of all other thoughts; therefore, if the self-conceit of the form of egoity which is the root of the illusory tree of *samsara* (bondage consisting of transmigration) is destroyed, all other thoughts will perish completely like an uprooted tree. Whatever thoughts arise as obstacles to one's *sadhana* (spiritual discipline), the mind should not be allowed to go in their direction, but should be made to rest in one's Self which is the *Atman*; one should remain as witness to whatever happens, adopting the attitude 'Let whatever strange things happen, happen; let us see!' This should be one's practice. In other words, one should not identify oneself with appearances; one should never relinquish one's Self. This is the proper means for destruction of the mind (*manonasa*) which is of the nature of seeing the body as Self, and which is the cause of all the aforesaid obstacles. This method which easily destroys egoity deserves to be called devotion (*bhakti*), meditation (*dhyana*), concentration (*yoga*), and knowledge (*jnana*). Because God remains of the nature of the Self, shining as 'I' in the heart, because the scriptures declare that thought itself is bondage, the best discipline is to stay quiescent without ever forgetting Him (God, the Self), after resolving in Him the mind which is of the form of the 'I'-thought, no matter by what means. This is the conclusive teaching of the Scriptures.

5

D: Is enquiry only the means for removal of the false belief of selfhood in the gross body, or is it also the means for removal of the false belief of selfhood in the subtle and causal bodies?

M: It is on the gross body that the other bodies subsist. In the false belief of the form 'I am the body' are included all the three bodies consisting of the five sheaths. And destruction of the false belief of selfhood in the gross body is itself the destruction of the false belief of selfhood in the other bodies. So enquiry is the means to removal of the false belief of selfhood in all the three bodies.

6

D: While there are different modifications of the internal organ, viz. *manas* (reflection), *buddhi* (intellect), *chitta* (memory) and *ahankara* (egoity), how can it be said that the destruction of the mind alone is release?

M: In the books explaining the nature of the mind, it is thus stated: "The mind is formed by the concretion of the subtle portion of the food we eat; it grows with the passions such as attachment and aversion, desire and anger; being the aggregate of mind, intellect, memory and egoity, it receives the collective singular name 'mind'; the characteristics that it bears are thinking, determining, etc.; since it is an object of consciousness (the self), it is what is seen, inert; even though inert, it appears as if conscious because of association with consciousness (like a red-hot iron ball); it is limited, non-eternal, partite, and changing like wax, gold, candle, etc.; it is of the nature of all elements (of phenomenal existence); its locus is the heart-lotus, even as the loci of the sense of sight, etc., are the eyes, etc.; it is the adjunct of the individual soul; thinking of an object, it transforms itself into a mode, and along with the knowledge that is in the brain, it flows through the five sense-channels, gets joined to objects by the brain (that is associated with knowledge), and thus knows and experiences objects and gains satisfaction. That substance is the mind." Even as one and the same person is called by different names according to the different functions he performs, so also one and the same mind is called by the different names: mind, intellect, memory, and egoity, on account of the difference in the modes – not because of any real difference. The mind itself is of the form of all, i.e. of soul, God and world; when it becomes of the form of the Self through knowledge there is release, which is of the nature of *Brahman*: this is the teaching.

7

D: If these four – mind, intellect, memory and egoity – are one and the same why are separate locations mentioned for them?

M: It is true that the throat is stated to be the location of the mind, the face or the heart of the intellect, the navel of the memory, and the heart or *sarvanga* of the egoity; though differently stated thus yet, for the aggregate of these, that is the mind or internal organ, the location is the heart alone. This is conclusively declared in the Scriptures.

8

D: Why is it said that only the mind which is the internal organ, shines as the form of all, that is of soul, God and world?

M: As instruments for knowing the objects the sense organs are outside, and so they are called outer senses; and the mind is called the inner sense because it is inside. But the distinction between inner and outer is only with reference to the body; in truth, there is neither inner nor outer. The mind's nature is to remain pure like ether. What is referred to as the heart or the mind is the collocation of the elements (of phenomenal existence) that appear as inner and outer. So there is no doubt that all phenomena consisting of names and forms are of the nature of mind alone. All that appear outside are in reality inside and not outside; it is in order to teach this that in the Vedas also all have been described as of the nature of the heart. What is called the heart is no other than *Brahman*.

9

D: How can it be said that the heart is no other than *Brahman*?

M: Although the self enjoys its experiences in the states of waking, dream, and deep sleep, residing respectively in the eyes, throat and heart, in reality, however, it never leaves its principal seat, the heart. In the heart-lotus which is of the nature of all, in other words in the mind-ether, the light of that self in the form 'I' shines. As it shines thus in everybody, this very self is referred to as the witness (*sakshi*) and the transcendent (*turiya*, literally the fourth). The 'I'-less supreme *Brahman* which shines in all bodies as interior to the light in the form 'I' is the Self-ether (or knowledge-ether): that alone is the Absolute Reality. This is the super-transcendent (*turiyatita*). Therefore, it is stated that what is called the heart is no other than *Brahman*. Moreover, for the reason that *Brahman* shines in the hearts of all souls as the Self, the name 'Heart' is given to *Brahman*.* The meaning of the word *hridayam*, when split thus '*hrit-ayam*', is in fact *Brahman*. The adequate evidence for the fact that *Brahman*, which shines as the Self, resides in the hearts of all is that all people indicate themselves by pointing to the chest when saying 'I'.

10

D: If the entire universe is of the form of mind, then does it not follow that the universe is an illusion? If that be the case, why is the creation of the universe mentioned in the Vedas?

M: There is no doubt whatsoever that the universe is the merest illusion. The principal purport of the Vedas is to make known the true *Brahman*, after showing the apparent universe to be false. It is for this purpose that the Vedas admit the creation of the world and not for any other reason. Moreover, for the less qualified persons creation is taught, that is the phased evolution of *prakriti* (primal nature), *mahat-tattva* (the great intellect), *tanmatras* (the subtle essences), *bhutas* (the gross elements), the world, the body, etc., from *Brahman*: while for the more qualified simultaneous creation is taught, that is, that this world arose like a dream on account of one's own thoughts induced by the defect of not knowing oneself as the Self. Thus, from the fact that the creation of the world has been described in different ways it is clear that the purport of the Vedas rests only in teaching the true nature of *Brahman* after showing somehow or other the illusory nature of the universe. That the world is illusory, every one can directly know in the state of realisation which is in the form of experience of one's bliss-nature.

---

* In the hearts of all individual souls, that which shines is Brahman and hence is called the Heart – *Brahma Gita*.

11

D: Is Self-experience possible for the mind, whose nature
is constant change?

M: Since *sattva guna* (the constituent of *prakriti* which
makes for purity, intelligence, etc.) is the nature of mind, and
since the mind is pure and undefiled like ether, what is called
mind is, in truth, of the nature of knowledge. When it stays in
that natural (i.e. pure) state, it has not even the name 'mind'. It
is only the erroneous knowledge which mistakes one for another
that is called mind. What was (originally) the pure *sattva*
mind, of the nature of pure knowledge, forgets its knowledge-
nature on account of nescience, gets transformed into the
world under the influence of *tamo guna* (i.e. the constituent of
prakriti which makes for dullness, inertness, etc.), being under
the influence of *rajo guna* (i.e. the constituent of *prakriti* which
makes for activity, passions, etc.), imagines 'I am the body,
etc.; the world is real', it acquires the consequent merit and
demerit through attachment, aversion, etc., and, through the
residual impressions (*vasanas*) thereof, attains birth and death.
But the mind, which has got rid of its defilement (sin) through
action without attachment performed in many past lives,
listens to the teaching of scripture from a true guru, reflects on
its meaning, and meditates in order to gain the natural state of
the mental mode of the form of the Self, i.e. of the form 'I am
Brahman' which is the result of the continued contemplation
of *Brahman*. Thus will be removed the mind's transformation
into the world in the aspect of *tamo guna*, and its roving therein
in the aspect of *rajo guna*. When this removal takes place the
mind becomes subtle and unmoving. It is only by the mind
that is impure and is under the influence of *rajas* and *tamas*
that Reality (i.e. the Self) which is very subtle and unchanging
cannot be experienced; just as a piece of fine silk cloth cannot

be stitched with a heavy crowbar, or as the details of subtle objects cannot be distinguished by the light of a lamp flame that flickers in the wind. But in the pure mind that has been rendered subtle and unmoving by the meditation described above, the Self-bliss (i.e. *Brahman*) will become manifest. As without mind there cannot be experience, it is possible for the purified mind endowed with the extremely subtle mode (*vritti*) to experience the Self-bliss, by remaining in that form (i.e. in the form of *Brahman*). Then, that one's self is of the nature of *Brahman* will be clearly experienced.

12

D: Is the aforesaid Self-experience possible, even in the state of empirical existence, for the mind which has to perform functions in accordance with its *prarabdha* (the past *karma* which has begun to fructify)?

M: A *brahmin* may play various parts in a drama; yet the thought that he is a *brahmin* does not leave his mind. Similarly, when one is engaged in various empirical acts there should be the firm conviction 'I am the Self', without allowing the false idea 'I am the body, etc.' to rise. If the mind should stray away from its state, then immediately one should enquire, 'Oh! Oh! We are not the body etc. Who are we?' and thus one should reinstate the mind in that (pure) state. The enquiry 'Who am I?' is the principal means to the removal of all misery and the attainment of the supreme bliss. When in this manner the mind becomes quiescent in its own state, Self-experience arises of its own accord, without any hindrance. Thereafter sensory pleasures and pains will not affect the mind. All (phenomena) will appear then, without attachment, like a dream. Never forgetting one's plenary Self-experience is real *bhakti* (devotion), *yoga*

(mind-control), *jnana* (knowledge) and all other austerities.
Thus say the sages.

13

D: When there is activity in regard to works, we are neither
the agents of those works nor their enjoyers. The activity is
of the three instruments (i.e., the mind, speech, and body).
Could we remain (unattached) thinking thus?

M: After the mind has been made to stay in the Self which
is its deity, and has been rendered indifferent to empirical
matters because it does not stray away from the Self, how can
the mind think as mentioned above? Do not such thoughts
constitute bondage? When such thoughts arise due to residual
impressions (*vasanas*), one should restrain the mind from
flowing that way, endeavour to retain it in the Self-state, and
make it turn indifferent to empirical matters. One should not
give room in the mind for such thoughts as: 'Is this good? Or,
is that good? Can this be done? Or, can that be done?' One
should be vigilant even before such thoughts arise and make the
mind stay in its native state. If any little room is given, such a
(disturbed) mind will do harm to us while posing as our friend;
like the foe appearing to be a friend, it will topple us down. Is
it not because one forgets one's Self that such thoughts arise
and cause more and more evil? While it is true that to think
through discrimination, 'I do not do anything; all actions are
performed by the instruments', is a means to prevent the mind
from flowing along thought *vasanas*, does it not also follow
that only if the mind flows along thought *vasanas* that it must
be restrained through discrimination as stated before? Can the
mind that remains in the Self-state think as 'I' and as 'I behave
empirically thus and thus'? In all manner of ways possible
one should endeavour gradually not to forget one's (true) Self

that is God. If that is accomplished, all will be accomplished. The mind should not be directed to any other matter. Even though one may perform, like a mad person, the actions that are the result of *prarabdha karma*, one should retain the mind in the Self-state without letting the thought 'I do' arise. Have not countless *bhaktas* (devotees) performed their numerous empirical functions with an attitude of indifference?

14

D: What is the real purpose of *sannyasa* (renunciation)?

M: *Sannyasa* is only the renunciation of the 'I'-thought, and not the rejection of the external objects. He who has renounced (the 'I'-thought) thus, remains the same whether he is alone or in the midst of the extensive *samsara* (empirical world). Just as when the mind is concentrated on some object, it does not observe other things even though they may be proximate, so also, although the sage may perform any number of empirical acts, in reality he performs nothing, because he makes the mind rest in the Self without letting the 'I'-thought arise. Even as in a dream one appears to fall head downwards, while in reality one is unmoving, so also the ignorant person, i.e., the person for whom the 'I'-thought has not ceased, although he remains alone in constant meditation, is in fact one who performs all empirical actions.* Thus the wise ones have said.

---

* Like those who listen to a story with their attention fixed elsewhere, the mind whose residual impressions have worn away does not really function even if it appears to do so. The mind that is not free from residual impressions really functions even if it does not appear to do so; this is like those who while remaining stationary imagine in their dreams that they climb up a hill and fall therefrom.

15

D: The mind, sense-organs, etc., have the ability to perceive; yet why are they regarded as perceived objects?

M:

	Drik (Knower)	Drisya (Known object)
1	The seer	Pot (i.e. the seen object)
	Further,	
2	The eye organ	Body, Pot, etc.
3	The sense of sight	The eye organ
4	The mind	The sense of sight
5	The individual soul	The mind
6	Consciousness (the Self)	The individual soul

As shown in the above scheme, since we, the consciousness, know all objects, we are said to be *drik* (knower). The categories ending with pot are the objects seen, since they are what are known. In the table of 'knowledge-ignorance (i.e. knower-known)' given above, among the knowers and objects of knowledge, it is seen that one is knower in relation to another; yet, since that one is object in relation to another, none of those categories is, in reality, the knower. Although we are said to be the 'knower' because we know all, and not the 'known' because we are not known by anything else, we are said to be the 'knower' only in relation to the known objects. In truth, however, what is called the 'known' is not apart from us. And so we are the Reality that transcends those two (the knower and the known). All the others fall within the knower-known categories.

16

D: How do egoity, soul, self, and *Brahman* come to be identified?

M:

The Example	The Exemplified
1 The iron-ball	Egoity
2 The heated iron-ball	The soul which appears as a superimposition on the Self
3 The fire that is in the heated iron-ball	The light of consciousness, i.e. the immutable *Brahman*, which shines in the soul in everybody
4 The flame of fire which remains as one	The all pervading *Brahman* which remains as one

From the examples given above, it will be clear how egoity, soul, witness, and All-witness come to be identified.

Just as in the wax-lump that is with the smith, numerous and varied metal-particles lie included and all of them appear to be one wax-lump, so also in deep sleep the gross and subtle bodies of all the individual souls are included in the cosmic *maya* which is nescience, of the nature of sheer darkness, and since the souls are resolved in the Self becoming one with it, they see everywhere darkness alone. From the darkness of sleep, the subtle body, viz. egoity, and from that (egoity) the gross body arise respectively. Even as the egoity arises, it appears superimposed on the nature of the Self, like the heated iron-ball. Thus, without the soul (*jiva*) which is the mind or egoity that is conjoined with the Consciousness-light, there is no witness of the soul, viz. the Self, and without the Self there is no *Brahman* that is the All-witness. Just as when the iron-ball is beaten into various shapes by the smith, the fire that is in it does not change thereby in any manner, even so the soul may be involved in ever so many experiences and undergo pleasures and pains, and yet the Self-light that is in it does not change in the least thereby, and like the ether it is the all-pervasive pure knowledge that is one, and it shines in the heart as *Brahman*.

17

D: How is one to know that in the heart the Self itself shines as *Brahman*?

M: Just as the elemental ether within the flame of a lamp is known to fill without any difference and without any limit both the inside and the outside of the flame, so also the knowledge-ether that is within the Self-light in the heart, fills without any difference and without any limit both the inside and the outside of that Self-light. This is what is referred to as *Brahman*.

18

D: How do the three states of experience, the three bodies, etc., which are imaginations, appear in the Self-light which is one, impartite and self-luminous? Even if they should appear, how is one to know that the Self alone remains ever unmoving?

M:

	The Example	The Exemplified
1	The Lamp	The Self
2	The door	Sleep
3	The door-step	*Mahat-tattva*
4	The inner wall	Nescience or the causal body

5	The mirror	The egoity
6	The windows	The five cognitive sense-organs
7	The inner chamber	Deep sleep in which the causal body is manifest
8	The middle chamber	Dream in which the subtle body is manifest
9	The outer court	Waking state in which the gross body is manifest

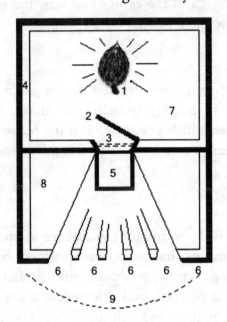

The Self which is the lamp (1) shines of its own accord in the inner chamber, i.e., the causal body (7) that is endowed with nescience as the inner wall (4) and sleep as the door (2); when by the vital principle as conditioned by time, *karma*, etc., the sleep-door is opened, there occurs a reflection of the Self in the egoity-mirror (5) that is placed next to the door-step – *Mahat-tattva*; the egoity-mirror thus illumines the middle chamber, i.e., the dream state (8), and, through the windows which are the five cognitive sense-organs (6), the outer court, i.e., the waking state. When, again, by the vital principle as conditioned by time, *karma*, etc., the sleep-door gets shut, the egoity ceases along with waking and dream, and the Self alone ever shines. The example just given explains how the Self is unmoving, how there is difference between the Self and the egoity and how the three states of experience, the three bodies, etc., appear.

19

D: Although I have listened to the explanation of the characteristics of enquiry in such great detail, my mind has not gained even a little peace. What is the reason for this?

M: The reason is the absence of strength or one-pointedness of the mind.

20

D: What is the reason for the absence of mental strength?

M: The means that make one qualified for enquiry are meditation, *yoga*, etc. One should gain proficiency in these through graded practice, and thus secure a stream of mental modes that is natural and helpful. When the mind that has in this manner become ripe, listens to the present enquiry, it will at once realise its true nature which is the Self, and remain in perfect peace, without deviating from that state. To a mind which has not become ripe, immediate realisation and peace are hard to gain through listening to enquiry. Yet, if one practises the means for mind-control for some time, peace of mind can be obtained eventually.

21

D: Of the means for mind-control, which is the most important?

M: Breath-control is the means for mind-control.

22

D: How is breath to be controlled?

M: Breath can be controlled either by absolute retention of breath (*kevala-kumbhaka*) or by regulation of breath (*pranayama*).

23

D: What is absolute retention of breath?

M: It is making the vital air stay firmly in the heart even without exhalation and inhalation. This is achieved through meditation on the vital principle, etc.

24

D: What is regulation of breath?

M: It is making the vital air stay firmly in the heart through exhalation, inhalation, and retention, according to the instructions given in the *yoga* texts.

25

D: How is breath-control the means for mind-control?

M: There is no doubt that breath-control is the means for mind-control, because the mind, like breath, is a part of air, because the nature of mobility is common to both, because the place of origin is the same for both, and because when one of them is controlled the other gets controlled.

26

D: Since breath-control leads only to quiescence of the mind (*manolaya*) and not to its destruction (*manonasa*), how can it be said that breath-control is the means for enquiry which aims at the destruction of mind?

M: The scriptures teach the means for gaining Self-realisation in two modes – as the *yoga* with eight limbs (*ashtanga yoga*) and as knowledge with eight limbs (*ashtanga-jnana*). By regulation of breath (*pranayama*) or by absolute retention thereof (*kevala kumbhaka*), which is one of the limbs of *yoga*, the mind gets controlled. Without leaving the mind at that, if one practises the further discipline such as withdrawal of the mind from external objects (*pratyahara*), then at the end, Self-realisation which is the fruit of enquiry will surely be gained.

27

D: What are the limbs of *yoga*?

M: *Yama, niyama, asana, pranayama, pratyahara, dharana, dhyana, and samadhi.* Of these –

(1) *Yama*: This stands, for the cultivation of such principles of good conduct as non-violence (*ahimsa*), truth (*satya*), non-stealing (*asteya*), celibacy (*brahmacharya*), and non-possession (*apari-graha*).

(2) *Niyama*: This stands for the observance of such rules of good conduct as purity (*saucha*), contentment (*santosha*), austerity (*tapas*), study of the sacred texts (*svadhyaya*), and devotion to God (*Isvara-pranidhana*).*

---

* The aim of *yama* and *niyama* is the attainment of all good paths open to those eligible for *moksha*. For more details see works like the *Yoga Sutra* and *Hathayoga Dipika*.

(3) *Asana*: Of the different postures, eightyfour are the main ones. Of these, again, four, viz. *simha, bhadra, padma,* and *siddha** are said to be excellent. Of these too, it is only *siddha,* that is the most excellent. Thus the *yoga* texts declare.

(4) *Pranayama*: According to the measures prescribed in the sacred texts, exhaling the vital air is *rechaka,* inhaling is *puraka* and retaining it in the heart is *kumbhaka.* As regards 'measure', some texts say that *rechaka* and *puraka* should be equal in measure, and *kumbhaka* twice that measure, while other texts say that if *rechaka* is one measure, *puraka* should be of two measures, and *kumbhaka* of four. By 'measure' what is meant is the time that would be taken for the utterance of the *Gayatri Mantra* once. Thus *pranayama* consisting of *rechaka, puraka,* and *kumbhaka,* should be practised daily according to ability, slowly and gradually. Then, there would arise for the mind a desire to rest in happiness without moving. After this, one should practise *pratyahara.*

(5) *Pratyahara*: This is regulating the mind by preventing it from flowing towards the external names and forms. The mind, which had been till then distracted, now becomes controlled. The aids in this respect are (1) meditation on the *pranava,* (2) fixing the attention betwixt the eyebrows, (3) looking at the tip of the nose, and (4) reflection on the *nada.* The mind that has thus become one-pointed will be fit to stay in one place. After this, *dharana* should be practised.

(6) *Dharana*: This is fixing the mind in a locus which is fit for meditation. The loci that are eminently fit for meditation are the heart and *Brahmarandhra* (aperture in the crown of the head). One should think that in the middle of the eight-

---

* *Siddhasana*: Left heel should be placed over the genital organ and over that, the right heel. Fixing one's gaze between the eyebrows one's body should be motionless and erect like a stick.

petalled lotus* that is at this place there shines, like a flame, the Deity which is the Self, i.e. *Brahman*, and fix the mind therein. After this, one should meditate.

(7) *Dhyana*: This is meditation, through the 'I am He' thought, that one is not different from the nature of the aforesaid flame. Even, thus, if one makes the enquiry 'Who am I?', then, as the Scripture declares, "The *Brahman* which is everywhere shines in the heart as the Self that is the witness of the intellect", one would realise that is the Divine Self that shines in the heart as 'I-I'. This mode of reflection is the best meditation.

(8) *Samadhi*: As a result of the fruition of the aforesaid meditation, the mind gets resolved in the object of meditation without harbouring the ideas 'I am such and such; I am doing this and this'. This subtle state in which even the thought 'I-I' disappears is *samadhi*. If one practises this every day, seeing to it that sleep does not supervene, God will soon confer on one the supreme state of quiescence of mind.

28

D: What is the purport of the teaching that in *pratyahara* one should meditate on the *pranava*?

M: The purport of prescribing meditation on the *pranava* is this. The *pranava* is *Omkara* consisting of three and a half *matras*, viz. *a, u, m,* and *ardha matra*. Of these, *a* stands for the waking state, *Visva jiva*, and the gross body; *u* stands for the dream-state *Taijasa jiva*, and the subtle body; *m* stands for the sleep-state, *Prajna jiva* and the causal body; the *ardha matra* represents the *Turiya* which is the self or 'I'-nature; and

---

* Although it is true that the lotus in the crown of the head is said to have a thousand petals, it also may be described as having eight petals because each of these eight consists of 125 sub-petals.

what is beyond that is the state of *Turiyatita*, or pure Bliss. The fourth state which is the state of 'I'-nature was referred to in the section on meditation (*dhyana*): this has been variously described – as of the nature of *amatra* which includes the three *matras*, *a*, *u*, and *m*; as *maunakshara* (silence-syllable); as *ajapa* (as muttering without muttering) and as the *Advaita mantra* which is the essence of all *mantras* such as *Panchakshara*. In order to get at this true significance, one should meditate on the *pranava*. This is meditation which is of the nature of devotion consisting in reflection on the truth of the Self. The fruition of this process is *samadhi* which yields release which is the state of unsurpassed bliss. The revered Gurus also have said that release is to be gained only by devotion which is of the nature of reflection on the truth of the Self.

29

D: What is the purport of teaching that one should meditate, through the 'I am He' thought, on the truth that one is not different from the self-luminous Reality that shines like a flame?

M: (A) The purport of teaching that one should cultivate the idea that one is not different from the self-luminous Reality is this: Scripture defines meditation in these words, "In the middle of the eight-petalled *heart-lotus* which is of the nature of all, and which is referred to as *Kailasa*, *Vaikunta*, and *Paramapada*, there is the Reality which is of the size of the thumb, which is dazzling like lightning and which shines like a flame. By meditating on it, a person gains immortality." From this we should know that by such meditation one avoids the defects of (1) the thought of difference, of the form 'I am different, and that is different', (2) the meditation on what is limited, (3) the idea that the real is limited, and (4) that it is confined to one place.

(B) The purport of teaching that one should meditate with the 'I am He' thought is this: *sahaham: soham; sah* the supreme Self, *aham* the Self that is manifest as 'I'. The *jiva* which is the *Sivalinga* resides in the heart-lotus which is its seat situated in the body which is the city of *Brahman*; the mind which is of the nature of egoity, goes outward identifying itself with the body, etc. Now the mind should be resolved in the heart, i.e. the I-sense that is placed in the body, etc., should be got rid of; when thus one enquires 'Who am I?', remaining undisturbed, in that state the Self-nature becomes manifest in a subtle manner as 'I-I'; that self-nature is all and yet none, and is manifest as the supreme Self everywhere without the distinction of inner and outer; that shines like a flame, as was stated above, signifying the truth 'I am *Brahman*'. If, without meditating on that as being identical with oneself, one imagines it to be different, ignorance will not leave. Hence, the identity-meditation is prescribed.

If one meditates for a long time, without disturbance, on the Self ceaselessly, with the 'I am He' thought which is the technique of reflection on the Self, the darkness of ignorance which is in the heart and all the impediments which are but the effects of ignorance will be removed, and the plenary wisdom will be gained.*

Thus, realising the Reality in the heart-cave which is in the city (of *Brahman*), viz. the body, is the same as realising the all-perfect God.

---

* If meditation in the form 'I am Siva' (*Sivoham bhavana*), which prevents the thought going outwards, is practised always, *samadhi* will come about – *Vallalar*.

In the city with nine gates, which is the body, the wise one resides at ease.*

The body is the temple; the *jiva* is God (*Siva*). If one worships him with the 'I am He' thought, one will gain release.

The body which consists of the five sheaths is the cave, the Supreme that resides there is the Lord of the cave. Thus the scriptures declare.

Since the Self is the reality of all the gods, the meditation on the Self which is oneself is the greatest of all meditations. All other meditations are included in this. It is for gaining this that the other meditations are prescribed. So, if this is gained, the others are not necessary. Knowing one's Self is knowing God. Without knowing one's Self that meditates, imagining that there is a deity which is different and meditating on it, is compared by the great ones to the act of measuring with one's foot one's own shadow, and to the search for a trivial conch after throwing away a priceless gem that is already in one's possession.†

30

D: Even though the heart and the *Brahmarandhra* alone are the loci fit for meditation, could one meditate, if necessary, on the six mystic centres (*adharas*)?

M: The six mystic centres, etc., which are said to be loci of meditation, are but products of imagination. All these are

---

* In the city that has nine false gates, He resides in the form of bliss – *Bhagavad Gita*.

† We shall meditate on that which, existing in the form of self, is the *atma-tattva*, is effulgent, and which residing in all living things always says "I", "I". To seek for a God outside, leaving the God residing in the cave of the heart, is like throwing away a priceless gem and searching for a trivial bead.

meant for beginners in *yoga*. With reference to meditation on
the six centres, the *Sivayogins* say, "God, who is of the nature of
the non-dual, plenary, Consciousness-Self, manifests, sustains
and resolves us all. It is a great sin to spoil that Reality by
superimposing on it various names and forms such as Ganapati,
Brahma, Vishnu, Rudra, Mahesvara and Sadasiva", and the
Vedantins declare, "All those are but imaginations of the mind."
Therefore, if one knows one's Self which is of the nature of
consciousness that knows everything, one knows everything.
The great ones have also said: "When that One is known as it
is in Itself, all that has not been known becomes known." If
we who are endowed with various thoughts meditate on God
that is the Self we would get rid of the plurality of thoughts
by that one thought; and then even that one thought would
vanish. This is what is meant by saying that knowing one's Self
is knowing God. This knowledge is release.

31

D: How is one to think of the Self?

M: The Self is self-luminous without darkness and light,
and is the reality which is self-manifest. Therefore, one should
not think of it as this or as that. The very thought of thinking
will end in bondage. The purport of meditation on the Self is
to make the mind take the form of the Self. In the middle of
the heart-cave the pure *Brahman* is directly manifest as the Self
in the form 'I-I'. Can there be greater ignorance than to think
of it in manifold ways, without knowing it as aforementioned?

32

D: It was stated that *Brahman* is manifest as the Self in the
form 'I-I', in the heart. To facilitate an understanding of this
statement, can it be still further explained?

M: Is it not within the experience of all that during deep sleep, swoon etc., there is no knowledge whatsoever, i.e. neither Self-knowledge nor other-knowledge? Afterwards, when there is experience of the form "I have woken up from sleep" or "I have recovered from swoon" – is that not a mode of specific knowledge that has arisen from the aforementioned distinctionless state? This specific knowledge is called *vijnana*. This *vijnana* becomes manifest only as pertaining to either the Self or the not-self, and not by itself. When it pertains to the Self, it is called true knowledge, knowledge in the form of that mental mode whose object is the Self, or knowledge which has for its content the impartite (Self); and when it relates to the not-self, it is called ignorance. The state of this *vijnana*, when it pertains to the Self and is manifest as of the form of the Self, is said to be the 'I'-manifestation. This manifestation cannot take place as apart from the Real (i.e. the Self). It is this manifestation that serves as the mark for the direct experience of the Real. Yet, this by itself cannot constitute the state of being the Real. That, depending on which this manifestation takes place is the basic reality which is also called *prajnana*. The *Vedantic* text "*prajnanam brahma*" teaches the same truth.

Know this as the purport of the scripture also. The Self which is self-luminous and the witness of everything manifests itself as residing in the *vijnanakosa* (sheath of the intellect). By the mental mode which is impartite, seize this Self as your goal and enjoy it as the Self.

33

D: What is that which is called the inner worship or worship of the attributeless?

M: In texts such as the *Ribhu Gita*, the worship of the attributeless has been elaborately explained (as a separate discipline). Yet, all disciplines such as sacrifice, charity, austerity, observance of vows, *japa, yoga* and *puja*, are, in effect, modes of meditation of the form 'I am Brahman'. So, in all the modes of disciplines, one should see to it that one does not stray away from the thought 'I am Brahman'. This is the purport of the worship of the attributeless.

34

D: What are the eight limbs of knowledge (*jnana-ashtanga*)?

M: The eight limbs are those which have been already mentioned, viz. *yama, niyama* etc., but differently defined:

(1) *Yama:* This is controlling the aggregate of sense- organs, realising the defects that are present in the world consisting of the body etc.

(2) *Niyama:* This is maintaining a stream of mental modes that relate to the Self and rejecting the contrary modes. In other words, it means love that arises uninterruptedly for the Supreme Self.

(3) *Asana:* That with the help of which constant meditation on *Brahman* is made possible with ease is *asana*.

(4) *Pranayama: Rechaka* (exhalation) is removing the two unreal aspects of name and form from the objects constituting the world, the body etc., *puraka* (inhalation) is grasping the three real aspects, existence, consciousness and bliss, which are constant in those objects, and *kumbhaka* is retaining those aspects thus grasped.

(5) *Pratyahara:* This is preventing name and form which have been removed from reentering the mind.

(6) *Dharana:* This is making the mind stay in the heart, without straying outward, and realising that one is the Self itself which is Existence-Consciousness-Bliss.

(7) *Dhyana:* This is meditation of the form 'I am only pure consciousness'. That is, after leaving aside the body which consists of five sheaths, one enquires 'Who am I?', and as a result of that, one stays as 'I' which shines as the Self.

(8) *Samadhi:* When the 'I'-manifestation also ceases, there is (subtle) direct experience. This is *samadhi*.

For *pranayama*, etc., detailed here, the disciplines such as *asana*, etc., mentioned in connection with *yoga* are not necessary. The limbs of knowledge may be practised at all places and at all times. Of *yoga* and knowledge, one may follow whichever is pleasing to one, or both, according to circumstances. The great teachers say that forgetfulness is the root of all evil, and is death for those who seek release,* so one should rest the mind in one's Self and should never forget the Self: this is the aim. If the mind is controlled, all else can be controlled. The distinction between *yoga* with eight limbs and knowledge with eight limbs has been set forth elaborately in the sacred texts; so only the substance of this teaching has been given here.

35

D: Is it possible to practise at the same time the *pranayama* belonging to *yoga* and the *pranayama* pertaining to knowledge?

M: So long as the mind has not been made to rest in the heart, either through absolute retention (*kevala-kumbhaka*) or through enquiry, *rechaka, puraka* etc., are needed. Hence, the *pranayama* of *yoga* is to be practised during training, and the other *pranayama* may be practised always. Thus, both may be practised. It is enough if the *yogic pranayama* is practised till skill is gained in absolute retention.

---

* Death or *Kala* is the giving up on this earth of the contemplation of the Self which should never be given up even the least bit – *Viveka Chudamani*.

36

D: Why should the path to release be differently taught? Will it not create confusion in the minds of aspirants?

M: Several paths are taught in the Vedas to suit the different grades of qualified aspirants. Yet, since release is but the destruction of mind, all efforts have for their aim the control of mind. Although the modes of meditation may appear to be different from one another, in the end all of them become one. There is no need to doubt this. One may adopt that path which suits the maturity of one's mind.

The control of *prana* which is *yoga*, and the control of mind which is *jnana**– these are the two principal means for the destruction of mind. To some, the former may appear easy, and to others the latter. Yet, *jnana* is like subduing a turbulent bull by coaxing it with green grass, while *yoga* is like controlling through the use of force. Thus the wise ones say: Of the three grades of qualified aspirants, the highest reach the goal by making the mind firm in the Self through determining the nature of the real by *Vedantic* enquiry and by looking upon one's self and all things as of the nature of the real; the mediocre by making the mind stay in the heart through *kevala kumbhaka* and meditating for a long time on the real; and the lowest grade, by gaining that state in a gradual manner through breath-control etc.

The mind should be made to rest in the heart till the destruction of the 'I'-thought which is of the form of ignorance, residing in the heart. This itself is *jnana*; this alone is *dhyana* also. The rest are a mere digression of words, digression from the texts. Thus the scriptures proclaim.

---

* Seeing everything as Real according to the Scripture: I am Brahman – one only without a second.

Therefore, if one gains the skill of retaining the mind in one's Self through some means or other, one need not worry about other matters.

The great teachers also have taught that the devotee is greater than the *yogins*** and that the means to release is devotion, which is of the nature of reflection on one's own Self.†

Thus, it is the path of realising *Brahman* that is variously called *Dahara vidya, Brahma vidya, Atma vidya* etc. What more can be said than this? One should understand the rest by inference.

The Scriptures teach in different modes. After analysing all those modes the great ones declare this to be the shortest and the best means.

37

D: By practising the disciplines taught above, one may get rid of the obstacles that are in the mind, viz. ignorance, doubt, error etc., and thereby attain quiescence of mind. Yet, there is one last doubt. After the mind has been resolved in the heart, there is only consciousness shining as the plenary reality. When thus the mind has assumed the form of the Self, who is there to enquire? Such enquiry would result in self-worship. It would be like the story of the shepherd searching for the sheep that was all the time on his shoulders!

M: The *jiva* itself is Siva; Siva Himself is the *jiva*. It is true that the *jiva* is no other than Siva. When the grain is

---

* Of all yogins, only he who rests his unwavering mind and love in me is dear to me – *Bhagavad Gita*.

† Of the means to release only *bhakti* (devotion) may be said to be the highest. For, *bhakti* is constant reflection on one's own Self – *Viveka Chudamani*.

hidden inside the husk, it is called paddy; when it is de-husked, it is called rice. Similarly, so long as one is bound by *karma* one remains a *jiva*; when the bond of ignorance is broken, one shines as Siva, the Deity. Thus declares a scriptural text. Accordingly, the *jiva* which is mind is in reality the pure Self; but, forgetting this truth, it imagines itself to be an individual soul and gets bound in the shape of mind. So its search for the Self, which is itself, is like the search for the sheep by the shepherd. But still, the *jiva* which has forgotten its self will not become the Self through mere mediate knowledge. By the impediment caused by the residual impressions gathered in previous births, the *jiva* forgets again and again its identity with the Self, and gets deceived, identifying itself with the body etc. Will a person become a high officer by merely looking at him? Is it not by steady effort in that direction that he could become a highly placed officer? Similarly, the *jiva*, which is in bondage through mental identification with the body etc., should put forth effort in the form of reflection on the Self, in a gradual and sustained manner; and when thus the mind gets destroyed, the *jiva* would become the Self.*

The reflection on the Self which is thus practised constantly will destroy the mind, and thereafter will destroy itself like the stick that is used to kindle the cinders burning a corpse. It is this state that is called release.

---

* Though the obstacles which cause the bondage of birth may be many, the root-cause for all such changes is *ahankara*. This root-cause must be destroyed for ever – *Viveka Chudamani.*

38

D: If the *jiva* is by nature identical with the Self, what is it that prevents the *jiva* from realising its true nature?

M: It is forgetfulness of the *jiva's* true nature; this is known as the power of veiling.

39

D: If it is true that the *jiva* has forgotten itself, how does the 'I'-experience arise for all?

M: The veil does not completely hide the *jiva;** it only hides the Self-nature of 'I' and projects the 'I am the body' notion; but it does not hide the Self's existence which is 'I', and which is real and eternal.

40

D: What are the characteristics of the *jivanmukta* (the liberated in life) and the *videhamukta* (the liberated at death)?

M: 'I am not the body. I am *Brahman* which is manifest as the Self. In me who am the plenary Reality,† the world consisting of bodies etc., are mere appearance, like the blue of the sky'. He who has realised the truth thus is a *jivanmukta*. Yet, so long as his mind has not been resolved, there may arise some misery for him because of relation to objects on account of *prarabdha* (*karma* which has begun to fructify and whose result is the present body), and as the movement of mind has not ceased there will not be also the experience of bliss. The experience of Self is possible only for the mind that has become subtle and

---

* Ignorance cannot hide the basic 'I', but it hides the specific truth that the *jiva* is the Supreme (Self).

† If there is prolonged meditation that the worlds are an appearance in me who am the plenary Reality, where can ignorance stand?

unmoving as a result of prolonged meditation. He who is thus endowed with a mind that has become subtle, and who has the experience of the Self is called a *jivanmukta*. It is the state of *jivanmukti* that is referred to as the attributeless *Brahman* and as the *Turiya*. When even the subtle mind gets resolved, and experience of self ceases, and when one is immersed in the ocean of bliss and has become one with it without any differentiated existence, one is called a *videhamukta*. It is the state of *videhamukti* that is referred to as the transcendent attributeless *Brahman* and as the transcendent *Turiya*. This is the final goal. Because of the grades in misery and happiness, the released ones, the *jivanmuktas* and *videhamuktas*, may be spoken of as belonging to four categories – *Brahmavid, Brahmavara, Brahmavariyan* and *Brahmavarishtha*. But these distinctions are from the standpoint of the others who look at them; in reality, however, there are no distinctions in release gained through *jnana*.

OBEISANCE

MAY THE FEET OF RAMANA, THE MASTER,
WHO IS THE GREAT SIVA HIMSELF,
WHO IS ALSO IN HUMAN FORM,
FLOURISH FOR EVER.

Om Tat Sat
Sri Ramanarpanamasthu